Meet the Orchestra

Written by **ANN HAYES**   Illustrated by **KARMEN THOMPSON**

Voyager Books • Harcourt, Inc.

Orlando Austin New York San Diego Toronto London

Requests for permission to make copies of any part of the work
should be mailed to the following address: Permissions Department,
Harcourt, Inc., 6277 Sea Harbor Drive, Orlando, Florida 32887-6777.

Voyager Books is a registered trademark of Harcourt, Inc.

Library of Congress Cataloging-in-Publication Data
Hayes, Ann.
Meet the orchestra/written by Ann Hayes; illustrated
by Karmen Effenberger Thompson.
p.   cm.
Summary: Describes the features, sounds and role of
each musical instrument in the orchestra.
ISBN: 0-15-200526-9
ISBN: 0-15-200222-7 (pbk.)
1. Orchestra—Juvenile literature. 2. Musical instruments—
Juvenile literature. [1. Orchestra. 2. Musical instruments.]
I. Thompson, Karmen Effenberger, ill. II. Title.
ML1200.H3 1990 784.19—dc20 89-32959

TWP   R Q P O

The paintings in this book were done in watercolor
on Arches cold press watercolor board.
The display type was set in ITC Korinna Kursiv
and the text type was set in Futura.
Color separations were made by Bright Arts, Ltd., Singapore.
Printed and bound by Tien Wah Press, Singapore
Production supervision by Warren Wallerstein and Ginger Boyer
Designed by Camilla Filancia

Printed in Singapore

For our parents:

HELEN and PENT EVERETT

and

CLAIRE and LEONARD DAVIDOW

with appreciation for their lifelong

encouragement and support

The Orchestra plays tonight. The audience has arrived. The musicians are coming on stage with their instruments. What a lot of different kinds they play—strings, woodwinds, brass, and percussion.

Violin

Players with like instruments sit together in "families." The violin belongs to the string family, along with the viola, the cello, and the big string bass. You play all of these with a bow or pluck them with your fingers.

The violin is the smallest of the string instruments. Its song can be bright as laughter, light as air, soft as a whisper, or sad as a tear.

Viola

As instruments get bigger, their voices get lower. The viola looks and sounds like a big brother to the violin. It has a deeper tone, reminding you of evening shadows, cloudy skies, and the color blue.

Cello

You can't tuck a cello under your chin the way you do a violin or viola. It is so big you must rest it on the floor. The cello's rich, mellow voice speaks of deep feelings like joy and sadness. It can remind you of the calm beauty of a drifting swan and of the color purple.

String Bass

The string bass is the grandpapa of the string family. It is so tall that you must stand up or sit on a high stool to play it.

When bowed, its low notes moan and groan. When plucked, its booming sound helps other musicians to keep the beat.

Flute

The flute belongs to the woodwind family, along with
the piccolo, oboe, bassoon, and clarinet. You blow
into these instruments to play them. At one time,
all of them were made of wood; today the flute
is often made of silver or even of gold.

To play the flute, you hold it sideways, tighten
your lips, and blow across the air hole. With
practice, you can trill like a bird or play slow,
quivering notes as cool as a mountain stream.

Piccolo

The piccolo, little sister to the flute,
loves attention and always gets it. This tiny
flute is so shrill you can't help hearing it.
Its high notes almost pierce your
eardrums. Yet everyone loves
the piccolo because it has
such a great sense
of fun.

Oboe

The oboe has a mouthpiece made of reed. The reed can be fussy and troublesome. Then it honks like a goose with a bad cold.

But usually the oboe can be trusted. The oboe plays that single note to which the whole orchestra tunes just before the concert begins. Its voice may remind you of faraway castles at sunset, autumn leaves, and the sadness of saying good-bye to someone you love.

Bassoon

The bassoon is like a large, folded oboe. It also has a reed mouthpiece. Its voice, like its name, has a kind of loneliness. Yet the bassoon can also be playful. It chats and chuckles with the other instruments. You often hear it chugging along like a tough little engine. Can't you almost see puffs of smoke coming out the top?

Clarinet

Here are two different clarinets. The straight one is nimble and quick. It tootles up and down the scale, never tripping over a note. Its cool tones melt in your ears just like ice cream melts in your mouth.

B-flat clarinet

This very long clarinet is bent at both ends so that it doesn't touch the floor when played. Its low, slow notes may remind you of clouds drifting across the moon or a snake swaying to a snake charmer's music.

bass clarinet

French Horn

Make way for the brass family, the powerhouse of the orchestra! Even when they play softly, you can sense a huge cat crouched to spring.

The brass do not have reed mouthpieces. Your lips buzzing against the metal mouthpiece produce the sound. The tubes of the horns magnify it, as a bullhorn magnifies an announcer's voice.

The French horn is like a big, bright bell at the end of a long, thin tube. The tube is coiled, so the horn can be played with one hand on the valves and the other inside the bell. The hand inside softens the sound. (Uncoiled, the French horn would reach all the way across a very large room. Someone would surely trip over it.)

The French horn has many voices. It can calm you with its gentle tones or thrill you with its gallant hunting call.

Trumpet

The trumpet's shorter tube makes it look easier to play than some of the fancier brass. But is it? No, say the trumpeters. You must work just as hard to learn it.

The trumpet's call is noble and exciting. It can remind you of flags flying, soldiers marching, and royal persons entering a great hall.

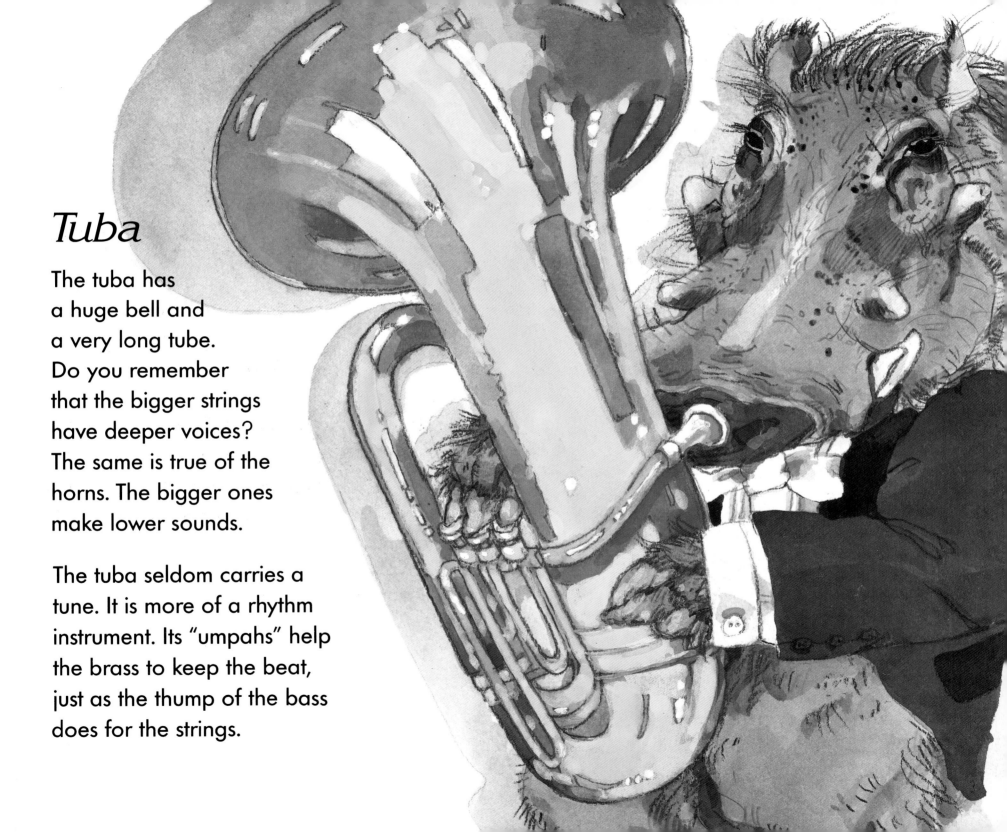

Tuba

The tuba has
a huge bell and
a very long tube.
Do you remember
that the bigger strings
have deeper voices?
The same is true of the
horns. The bigger ones
make lower sounds.

The tuba seldom carries a
tune. It is more of a rhythm
instrument. Its "umpahs" help
the brass to keep the beat,
just as the thump of the bass
does for the strings.

Timpani or Kettledrums

The big kettledrums sit in the "kitchen," or percussion section of the orchestra. Everything that is beaten, banged, dinged, or pinged belongs there.

Have you ever heard the orchestra rumble with the sound of distant thunder? Suddenly it explodes with a "BOOM-BOOM-BOOM!" That is the timpani. They look like big kettles sitting side by side. Each has a slightly different pitch. You beat rapidly from one to another, making the thunder crash and roll.

Cymbals

The cymbals look like a pair of pot lids. When banged together, they crash with the fury of an electric storm. If the kettledrums give you the roll of thunder, the cymbals give you the flash of lightning. Hear them ring out just when the music reaches a peak of excitement. This is a proud moment for the whole orchestra!

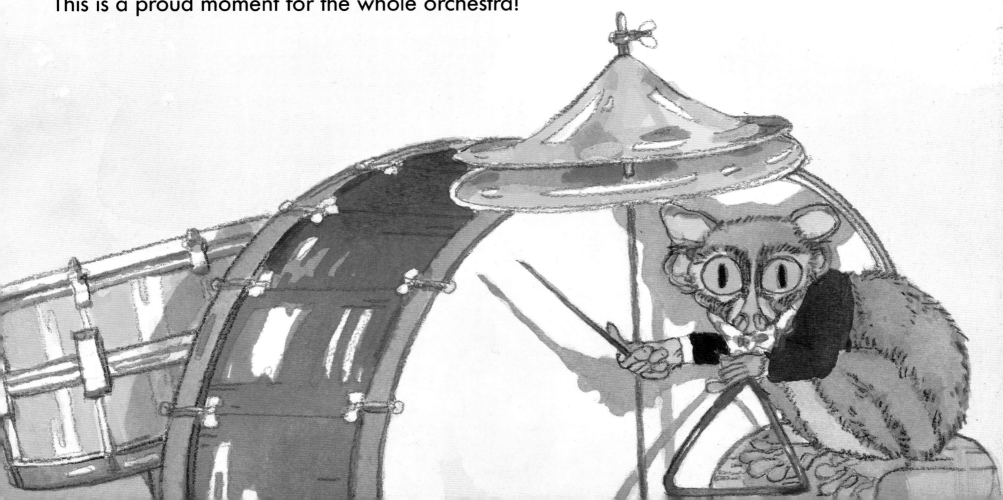

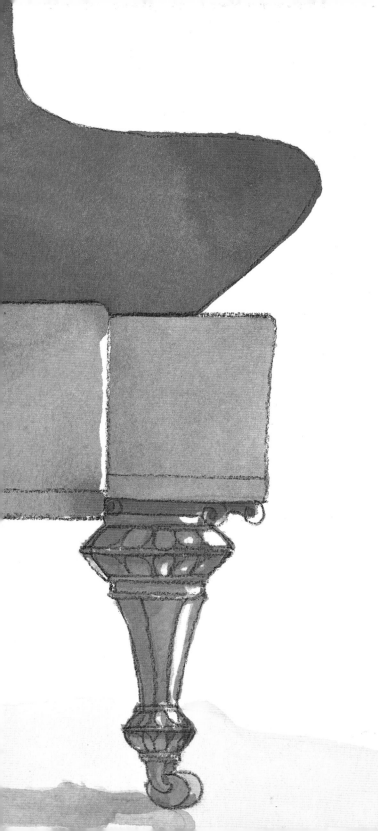

Piano

When you sit down at the piano, the black
and white keys make your fingers want to dance.
From the center you can play them all—the high
ones on your right and the low ones on your left.

When you hear a murmur of notes burst into
thundering chords, then fade into silence, it is
probably the voice of the piano. When it is over,
you may want to clap—or perhaps even cry.

Conductor

Now, meet the conductor. He is often called "maestro," which means master of the orchestra. That he is, for he leads the musicians at all times. He does it mostly by talking with his hands! In his right hand he holds a small stick—the baton. With it he beats time. His left hand motions, "You play now!" "Be quick!" "Livelier!" "Louder!" "Softer!" "Ah, that's perfect!" A raised eyebrow says, "You're playing off key!"

The musicians have taken their places. The strings, who are by far the largest group of players, sit in front, almost filling the stage. The woodwinds sit close together at the center. The brass and percussion are in back.

The conductor strides on stage in front of the orchestra, raises his baton . . .

Let the music start!

The orchestra played tonight. Now it is time
to go home. Like the voices of their instruments,
the musicians drift off into the night.